RADIO

Rebecca Coyle

The Media

Advertising
Book Publishing
Cinema
Magazines
The Pop Music Business
Newspapers
Radio
Television and Video

Series designer: David Armitage
Series editor: Susannah Foreman
Picture research: Elizabeth Miller

Cover: *Ed Stewart, radio presenter for
Radio Mercury and BBC Radio 2.*

First published in 1988 by
Wayland (Publishers) Ltd
61 Western Road, Hove
East Sussex BN3 1JD, England

© Copyright 1988 Wayland (Publishers) Ltd

Phototypeset by Direct Image Photosetting,
Hove, East Sussex
Printed in Italy by G. Canale & C.S.p.A., Turin
Bound in France by AGM

British Library Cataloguing in Publication Data

Coyle, Rebecca
    Radio. — (The media).
    1. Radio — Juvenile literature
    I. Title   II. Series
    621.3841   TK6550.7

ISBN 1-85210-238-1

Contents

Introduction

Radio is a medium we use constantly, although we may not even be aware of it. We may use it as background entertainment while we do something else, or we may become totally involved as we listen to our favourite programme. Most of us depend on the radio for news of what is happening locally and around the world. The major reason for radio's widespread appeal is that it is portable. Small, lightweight radios powered by batteries can be carried around easily, so we can listen to radio wherever we go.

Radio programmes are relatively simple to produce. Broadcast equipment is not very complicated to operate, so production skills are easily acquired. Nor is radio broadcasting hampered by high production costs. Radio makes pictures in our minds, not before our eyes, and therefore does not need to provide expensive sets and costumes. In fact, one of the most exciting aspects of radio is the way it can fire our imaginations.

Radio is the oldest broadcast medium and every country in the world has at least one radio station. In Britain it is estimated that 90 per cent of the adult population listens to radio. Radio is a warm, personal means of communication. Listeners describe it as 'a welcome distraction', like a friend, and enjoy it because it allows them to get involved. It can involve us either as listeners or as programmers. Radio, the medium that offers immediate news, information and entertainment, has become an important part of our daily lives.

Radio can be with us wherever we go. Personal stereo radio and cassette units are compact, lightweight and cheap to buy. Some are no bigger than a pocket calculator.

1 The history of Radio

There is no single person who is the inventor of radio as we know it today. Its development, like most inventions, is based on the theories and contributions of many people. The existence of radio waves was first predicted in 1864 by the English physicist, James Clerk Maxwell. In 1888, a German physicist, Heinrich Hertz, demonstrated that radio waves actually do exist and that they travel through space. Many attempts were made to communicate via radio waves; but the most successful of the radio pioneers was an Italian, Guglielmo Marconi. Marconi used radio waves to send dot-and-dash codes like those used in telegraphs, but using radio waves, not wires.

This new method of communication, which came to be known as the 'wireless', was to revolutionize communication. Before its development, the only means of quick, long-distance communication was the telegraph and the telephone. But the signals sent by both these devices had to travel through wires. This meant that communication was possible only between places that were connected by wires. Radio signals, on the other hand, passed through the air, making it possible to communicate between any two points on land, sea, and later in the sky and even in space.

Marconi moved to England — at that time one of the greatest shipping countries in the world — and set up the Marconi Company to develop the wireless for ship-to-shore and ship-to-ship communication. This was the first major use of the wireless and is still an important use today. In 1901 Marconi was successful in sending the first wireless message across the Atlantic, from Cornwall to Newfoundland, a distance of 3,000 miles.

Marconi's wireless could transmit only dot-and-dash codes, not spoken messages. Voice transmission became possible with the

Guglielmo Marconi with his 'black box' radio. In 1896 Marconi demonstrated its use by sending signals between two post offices in the City of London.

Listening to radio using headphones and a crystal set in the 1920s. Families used to gather round to listen to radio attached to loudspeakers.

development of the vacuum tube, which was able to amplify (increase) the sound signals. The vacuum tube was first developed in 1904 by John Ambrose Fleming, an English engineer. This tube was a diode, which means it had two electrical parts. In 1906, an American, Lee De Forest, added a third part to Fleming's tube to make the triode valve. The triode vacuum tube paved the way for radio broadcasting. The word 'broadcasting', which originally meant to scatter or sow seeds over a wide area, was first used in the USA to describe transmitting voices by wireless.

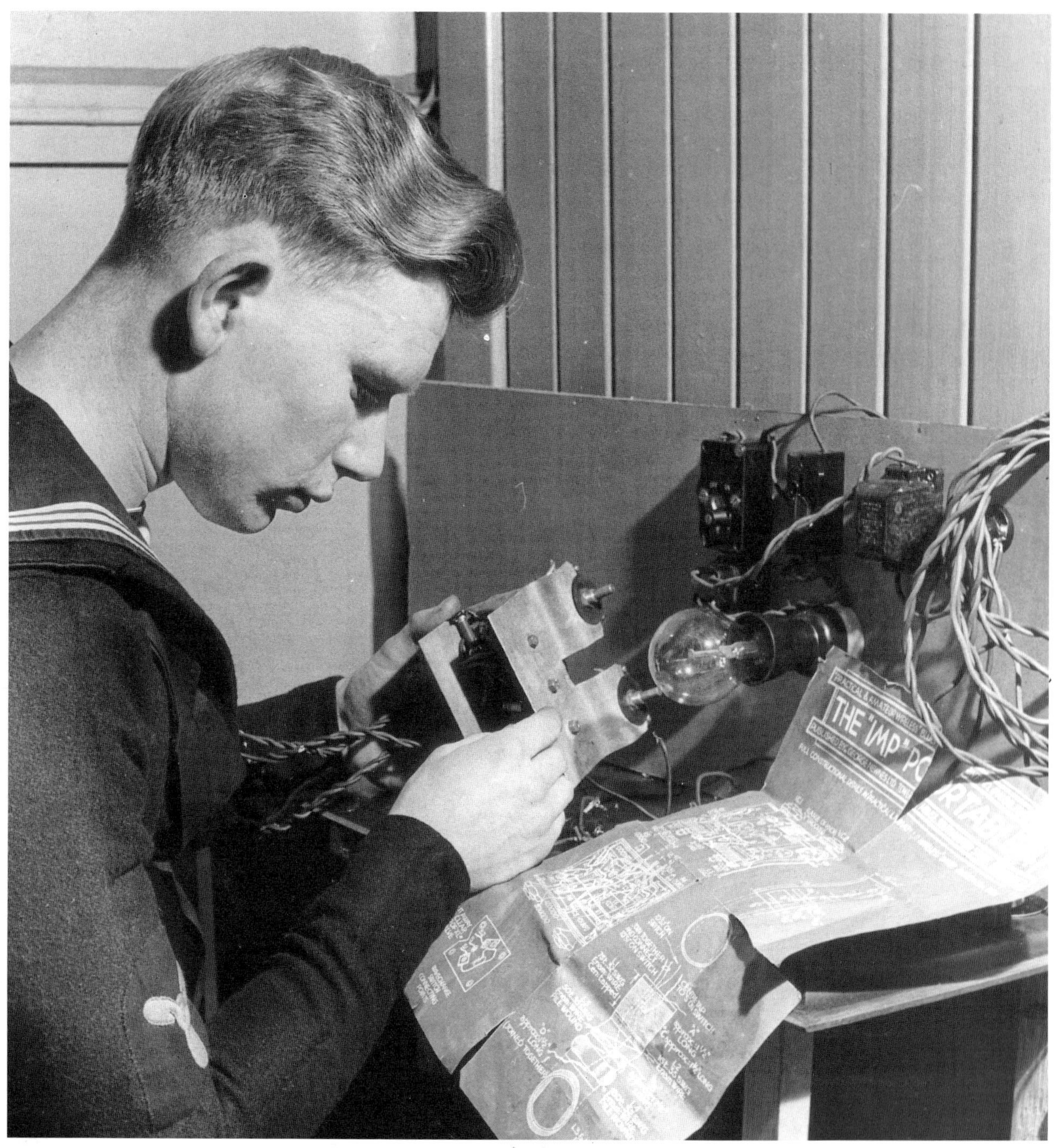

The first radio broadcast was sent out by Reginald Fessenden from his experimental radio station in Massachusetts, USA on Christmas Eve, 1906. The programme consisted of musical selections, poems and readings from the Bible, and was received by surprised wireless operators on ships within a radius of several hundred miles. Fessenden continued to make frequent music and talk

Ex-servicemen who had learned how to use radio in the First World War started up their own experimental radio stations as a hobby.

broadcasts until 1916 when the USA entered the First World War, and the use of the wireless was restricted to military purposes.

After the relaxation of military restrictions on radio at the conclusion of the First World War in

1918, many experimental radio stations were set up by ex-servicemen and other amateurs who were skilled in the use of wireless. These early transmitting stations were usually equipped with home-made apparatus, and radio receiving sets were mostly in the hands of other experimenters who pursued the use of radio as a hobby. But as interest grew, and more and more people wanted to hear music and news from the air, permanent stations, built specially for radio broadcasting, were set up.

The first radio station to be licensed by the US government was KDKA in Pittsburgh, a station owned by the Westinghouse Company. It went on the air on 2 November 1920 with the broadcast of the returns of the presidential election. This was the start of wireless fever in the USA. The success of the KDKA broadcast and the music programmes it initiated motivated others to establish similar stations. By November 1922, two years after KDKA's first broadcast, there were 564 licensed stations in the USA. In May 1927, millions of listeners heard the radio coverage of Charles Lindbergh's solo flight across the Atlantic.

The 'Golden Age of Radio' in the USA from 1934 to 1941 meant the development of many different forms of popular programmes. Salon orchestras, political and sports reporting, voices of famous people as well as the rise in popularity of entertainment personalities were the most significant areas of expansion. Jack

This 1940s ECME radio set was manufactured in just 30 minutes in a robot plant and cost one-fifth of the usual price.

Benny, Eddie Cantor, Amos 'n' Andy, George Burns and Gracie Allen became better known as radio entertainers than they had been in theatre, film or vaudeville. Radio drama such as The Shadow and The Lone Ranger, soap operas, children's shows, quizzes and audience participation shows all created new forms of entertainment. Controversial issues were discussed in a modified debate covering a variety of viewpoints on Town Meeting of the Air.

The early radio stations were able to cover the operating costs of broadcasting with profits from the sale of receiving sets, which were in great demand in the 1920s. They also sold airtime to people who wanted to put out their own messages. But the value of radio as an advertising medium soon became apparent, and eventually, advertising became the principal means of support for broadcasting in the USA.

In Britain radio's history took a different course. The government became concerned over the use of radio during the Easter 1916 Dublin Uprising in Ireland. Rebels had seized the central Post Office and transmitted their own radio reports of the uprising to the outside world. As a result, the British government imposed strict controls on the use of wireless broadcasts.

In 1919 the Marconi Company began daily broadcasts of speech and music, including a well-received broadcast by the Australian opera singer Dame Nellie Melba. But in 1920, opposition from the armed services, who feared interference with essential communication, and the general desire to avoid the commercialization of radio led to a ban on the Marconi broadcasts.

Lord Reith locking up Savoy Hill after the last programme was broadcast from there. The BBC then moved to Broadcasting House, where many of its radio services are still based.

During the Great Depression of the 1930s President Roosevelt spoke about government policies to the people of the USA in what became known as 'Fireside Chats'.

Nevertheless, interest in this new medium continued to grow, and in 1922 amateur radio enthusiasts, grouped together into 63 societies with a total membership of about 3,000, petitioned the government to lift the ban and allow regular broadcasts. Their request was partially granted; the Marconi Company was allowed to broadcast half an hour a week, with a break every three minutes for the operator to listen for official messages.

Other companies requested permission to broadcast and to manufacture radio sets, and the government persuaded them to form an organization called the British Broadcasting Company (BBC). The company began operating in 1922 and appointed John C.W. Reith (later Lord Reith) as managing director. BBC programmes included music, drama and comedy, a children's hour and religious and school broadcasts. Within three years a national network had been established, and by 1925 reception was available to 85 per cent of the population, often with the choice of national and regional programmes.

In 1927, the BBC became the British Broadcasting Corporation, whose aim was to provide wireless broadcasting as a general public service. John Reith became the director-general of the BBC and declared that wireless programming should 'inform, educate and entertain'. Sunday broadcasts were mainly

In Germany in the 1930s the Nazis used radio transmitters to broadcast Adolf Hitler's powerful speeches at European rallies.

By 1939, 30 per cent of British audiences were listening to illegal broadcasts by Lord Haw Haw, a propagandist working for the Germans.

religious services, talks and classical music. In the early 1930s, two European-based commercial radio stations, Radio Normandie and Radio Luxembourg, offered British audiences American-style programmes, including soap operas and light music. On Sundays more listeners tuned into these stations than to the BBC.

Radio also became used for political messages. In 1933, the first of US President Franklin D. Roosevelt's famous 'Fireside Chats' was broadcast to the people of the USA during the difficult days of the Depression. In Italy, leader of the authoritarian nationalistic fascist party, Benito Mussolini, broadcast political messages or propaganda. Over Europe via short-wave broadcasts, Adolf Hitler's speeches encouraged the growth of the fascist movement. During the Spanish Civil War, shocking propaganda broadcasts by General Queipo de Llano via a huge radio transmitter supplied by the Germans encouraged the nationalist struggle for power. In 1939 William Joyce, an Englishman known as Lord Haw Haw, broadcast propaganda to the British, calling for support for Nazi Germany.

When the Second World War broke out in 1939, the BBC combined its national and regional programmes into a single Home Service. In 1940, to maintain the morale of troops in France, it introduced the Forces Programme. Mainly an entertainment service, this featured dance music, sport and variety. Within the next two years, the Forces Programme grew to be more popular than the Home Service with both civilians and servicemen. The war years were important in the development of the BBC's news coverage. Huge audiences listened to the BBC 9 pm news bulletin, and a particular format emerged: a combination of reading, correspondents' reports from the war zones and actual sound (actuality) from the news locations. Prime Minister Winston Churchill regularly broadcast messages on the development of the war to the nation.

After the war, the Home Service continued as a basic London service, which the regional services — Scottish, Northern, Midland, Welsh, West and Northern Irish — could draw upon. The Forces Programme was replaced in 1945 by a very similar Light Programme. The Third Programme, offering arts coverage, serious discussion and experiment, began in 1946. Radio popularity was at its peak in Britain, with the development of current affairs, debates, drama and popular serials, light entertainment and comedy, and classical and popular music.

Meanwhile the USA was taking another approach to broadcasting. By the end of the war, 800 radio stations served troops overseas and a distinctive pop music, commercial style had emerged. Another form of radio was established in 1948 with KPFA broadcasting from Berkeley, California. KPFA was (and still is) run by and paid for by listener supporters, many of whom were social activists. The mid-1960s saw a rapid growth in this type of operation, called community radio.

The introduction of television drastically undermined radio's popularity. Between 1949 and 1958, the BBC's average evening radio audience dropped from nearly 9 million to less than 3.5 million, three-quarters of whom were people without television sets. This decline in popularity was, in part, due to the generally conservative nature of BBC radio programmes.

Then the 'pirate' radio stations began to appear, illegally broadcasting music from record companies not played elsewhere. These

Above *Prime Minister Churchill broadcast information and reassuring messages to the British people during and after the Second World War.*

Above *BBC news reporters describing a dogfight during the Battle of Britain, in 1940.*

stations ran on funds provided by the music industry and advertising fees from small firms who could not afford national or regional advertising for their local shop or service. In 1964, Radio Caroline began broadcasting from

a ship off the English Essex coast. In its first three weeks, the station gained 7 million listeners to its popular music programme. By 1967, nine ships and forts were on air as pirate stations. To stem this growth, the government passed the Marine Offences Act which outlawed supplying to or advertising on ship radio stations. This led to the closure of off-shore pirates for a short while.

In 1967, the BBC responded to the popularity of pirate programmes by setting up a continuous pop music network called Radio 1. Meanwhile, the Light, Third and Home continued as mixed programme networks and became Radios 2, 3 and 4. It was not until 1970 that Radio 2 became a network for continuous 'middle-of-the-road' music; Radio 3 broadcast classical music; and Radio 4 took on general entertainment, specializing in informational or 'spoken word' output.

During the late 1960s, regional radio was gradually replaced by local radio. The first BBC local radio station started broadcasting in

Above *The offshore 'pirate' station, Radio Caroline, evades the 1967 Maritime Act by broadcasting from outside British waters.*

Below *DJ Robin Scott at Capital Radio. This independent local radio station broadcasts chart music to young London audiences.*

Volunteer reporters in Australian public radio station 3CR broadcast views and voices often unheard on other services.

Radio signals sent and received on specially allocated VHF frequencies are used for emergency services such as mountain rescue teams.

Leicester in 1967, and many other local stations were established during the 1970s and 1980s. The phone-in show, first used in 1969, was a broadcasting technique developed by local radio. In 1973, the first independent local radio (ILR) stations, Capital Radio and the London Broadcasting Company (LBC), began operating in London. These and other independent local radio stations are financed by income from advertisements on air and are regulated by the Independent Broadcasting Authority (IBA). They broadcast a mixture of local and networked news and information, phone-ins and pop music.

Though Britain's ILR stations operate on a local basis, they do not have the mechanisms to allow a wide cross-section of the population to make programmes, to have their voices heard on radio or to be part of how the station operates. But there are truly representative community radio stations operating in other countries. In the USA, the National Federation of Community Broadcasters was set up in 1975. In Australia, community radio (called 'public radio') was introduced in the early 1970s, and there are now over 70 stations broadcasting.

In Britain, the lack of community access and the inability of local radio services to represent certain segments of society, resulted in the growth of pirate radio during the 1970s and the 1980s, and pirate stations now flourish in Britain despite continual raids by government agencies. The government proposed an experiment in community radio in 1985 but they cancelled it at the last minute, preferring to wait until a general review of radio was completed.

Besides these overhead-transmitting radio services, there are other forms of radio that broadcast to a small area via cables. For example, hospital radio, started in Britain in 1951, can be received through patient headphones. In 1976, the Home Office set up an experiment in cable radio and television transmitting on housing estates in eleven new towns. Two of these still operate. Large department stores and businesses also have a form of cable radio for customers and workers, and there are student radio stations operating on campuses throughout the world.

There is also a form of point-to-point communication known as CB, or Citizens' Band, that allows messages to be sent to and received by individual radio operators over a certain distance. CB has been established in the USA since 1947. In Britain, it was not until 1981 that CB was legalized.

2 How radio works

Radio broadcasting originates at the radio studio where a microphone picks up the various sounds and converts them into electrical sound signals. These signals are sent by cable to a radio transmitting tower. Here the signals are amplified and travel on invisible radio waves, radiating in all directions from the transmitting aerial. All radio sets have a receiving aerial that picks up signals and converts them back into sound. The receiving aerial may be an outside rod or wire, or a special aerial built inside portable receivers. Radio was first listened to on headphones attached to crystal set receivers. Later, with the invention of valve receivers with loudspeakers, headphones were no longer necessary. Modern portable receivers are equipped with small transistor elements that amplify the sound. Receivers are also equipped with a tuning device that can be adjusted to receive the frequency of a particular station and shut out others.

Radio waves radiate in all directions from their source. They travel through space in much the same way as water waves travel when a pebble is dropped into a pond. Although radio waves are invisible, the length of a radio wave can be measured with scientific instruments. Wavelength determines the frequency of a wave, i.e. the number of waves that travel past a point in one second. If a wave is long, the crests of the wave are far apart and follow one another slowly. If a wave is short, the crests are close together and follow one another quickly. Therefore long waves are of low frequency, and short waves are of high frequency. The frequency of radio waves is referred to as Hertz (abbreviated as Hz), to commemorate the contributions of Heinrich Hertz to the development of radio. Radio stations in Britain use mostly medium-frequency waves, or mega-Hertz (mHz), called MW. Many stations in the

Above *With greater access to the airwaves, many cities in the USA have hundreds of local stations broadcasting via transmitters like these.*

Radio receivers have tuning controls that enable us to select the frequency for each station, which can be VHF, MW or LW.

Above *Walkie-talkie radios are two-way communication systems used by police and other authorities.*

USA use Very High Frequency (VHF), called FM, to give a clear signal for music broadcasts. Low frequency waves, or kilo-Hertz (kHz), are the most common, used by stations around the world. They are referred to as LW or AM.

Radio frequencies are allocated to each country by the International Telecommunications Union, an international organization that controls the use of radio air space. According to international agreement, countries are assigned 'call letters' by which their broadcast stations can be identified. In the USA, for example, the assigned call letters are K or W, so all stations' identification codes start with either K or W. Pirate stations that broadcast illegally choose their own frequency and sometimes use one already allocated, thereby blocking or interfering with another station. Some frequencies are reserved for navigation, for international telephone and telegraph, and

Compact, lightweight, relatively inexpensive cassette recorders are now used for interviewing by amateur and professional radio reporters.

for use by police and military authorities.

With advances in modern technology, radio stations are able to use fairly simple and easy-to-operate equipment. New developments have meant that portable recorders for interviewing and recording sounds from a particular place are becoming smaller and cheaper. In the past, radio reporters had to rely on bulky open-reel recorders that used quarter-inch tape for on-the-spot interviews. Now they use high-quality cassette recorders, some of them little bigger than a personal cassette player. Another major development in radio and television technology is the use of satellites orbiting in space. Audio/visual signals are sent to the satellite and bounced back to other parts of the world almost simultaneously, making it possible to broadcast 'live' from one country to another.

In Britain, all legal public radio broadcasting is controlled and financed by either the BBC (British Broadcasting Corporation) or the IBA (Independent Broadcasting Authority). Both these bodies are responsible to Parliament through the Home Secretary. Under the Wireless Telegraphy Act, the Home Secretary has the power to remove their licences to broadcast. Both the BBC and the IBA are controlled by boards composed of people chosen by the Home Secretary to represent the 'public interest'. Until recently, many of these people were chosen for their rank and title

rather than for their understanding of broadcasting and relevant experience.

The major difference between the BBC and the IBA is that the BBC is responsible for everything to do with radio (and television) broadcasts including programme production. The IBA does not actually *make* programmes; it awards contracts or 'franchises' to commercial radio (and television) companies. These companies must pay rental to the IBA for the use of its transmitters.

BBC services are financed directly by the

Above *The Yukon Territory local radio station in Canada relays broadcasts from the Canadian Broadcasting Corporation to this remote community.*

Below *An engineer at the control desk of a local independent radio station. On-air advertisements finance the station.*

public through the television licence fee. This pays for television as well as for national Radios 1, 2, 3 and 4, the regional networks of Scotland, Wales and Northern Ireland, and local radio. Independent Radio stations (IBA services) are paid for indirectly by the public through advertising. Radio programmes on independent stations can include up to nine minutes of advertising each hour. Advertisers cover the cost of these commercials by increasing the price of their products. When we buy the product, we help to pay for its advertising, which in turn, is a major source of financing for commercial stations.

Even though we pay, either directly or indirectly, for broadcasting, it is often difficult to have a say in what is broadcast, who broadcasts and how radio broadcasts are made. In Britain, regular public meetings are held to allow listeners to voice their opinions. These meetings can be quite intimidating, however. Officially the government does not become involved in broadcasting; but it can apply pressure to governing bodies to ban programmes it feels may, for instance, threaten national security or the status quo.

In the USA, there has never been a national broadcasting organization similar to the BBC. There are about 10,000 radio stations and, of these, around 1,900 are non-commercial; that is, they get financial support from listeners, businesses, local or central government grants or other organizations. In 1967, the Corporation for Public Broadcasting was set up to provide government funding for non-commercial stations, which may be community, educational or public radio stations. Other stations are

Australian public radio station 3CR's new building and studios were financed by a 'Friends of 3CR' Trust with listener and station worker shareholders.

financed largely through advertising. The Federal Communications Commission allocates available frequencies to radio stations and issues licences to broadcast.

In Australia, the Australian Broadcasting Commission (ABC) provides national, regional and overseas short-wave (as well as television) services. The ABC is funded directly through the government treasury, which means the public pays for it through income tax. There are also commercial radio stations run on income from advertising and organized under the Federation of Australian Radio Broadcasters. The Special Broadcasting Service operates two 'ethnic' radio stations, which broadcast over Melbourne and Sydney in up to 40 different languages. Australia has a third tier of radio called Public Broadcasting, which is supported by the Public Broadcasting Association of Australia. There are about 70 of these types of stations.

The basic aims of a station, whether primarily to make money or to provide airtime for people not heard, affect the way programmes are made. For example, regulatory bodies may require a certain percentage of 'community service' or 'educational' programming. While all stations operate within specific budgets, if they have to make large profits for their shareholders, then programmes that are expensive to produce, such as radio drama and documentaries, may not be commissioned. These aspects link together in the overall operation of a station.

3 Inside the radio station

A radio broadcasting station operating commercially is much the same the world over. Putting a show on the air involves many different types of skills and functions. In small stations one person may do many jobs that in a large station are the responsibility of a whole department. But for all stations, the key people are the station manager, who usually has a general idea of everything that is going on in the station, and the programme co-ordinator, who recommends to the station manager which programmes to broadcast and takes responsibility for the programme schedule.

A different group of people actually produce the programmes. The producer sees to the overall format of the programme, deciding order of items, their length and style of presentation. If the programme has a large budget, a

Above *Reading the news in a production studio. This is linked to the main on-air studio through one of the control desk channels.*

Below *In the studio, the presenter talks while the producer in the 'cubicle' co-ordinates each item.*

The heart of the station is the main technical equipment or 'racks' room. Everything broadcast is recorded or 'logged' on open-reel tape.

researcher may provide background information and a production assistant/secretary may assist the producer. In a large station there may be several producers, each with overall responsibility for specific programmes, e.g. music, art or sports programmes. The presenter, or disc jockey (DJ) for music programmes, is the one to put the ideas over on the air. Other production staff will produce the advertisement and station 'jingles'.

The news gathering is an important function of any radio station, and in some large stations is the work of a separate department with a team to report, edit, and read the news. Small stations may have just one person to do all this and, therefore, may rely on local newspapers and networked news sent out from a central source such as Independent Radio News (IRN). Large stations often have reporters in other cities and countries who telephone in their news reports.

The engineering, or technical, staff makes sure that the sound signals get from the radio station to the transmitter. The engineer ensures that the sound is properly mixed and brings outside broadcasts (OBs) into the studio. These may come from radio cars, concert halls or other public places.

A commercial station needs to make money to pay for its production costs. The advertising staff raise money by selling advertising airtime to businesses and other organizations. Much of their work depends on audience research into programme and presenter popularity and listening time preferences. The most popular listening times, such as breakfast time, are known as 'peak times' and have the highest advertising rates and the most popular programmes and presenters.

Advertisements, jingles and community announcements are kept on loops of tape called cartridges that do not need rewinding and are kept close at hand.

The public relations staff ensure that the radio station has a high profile in the community. Often a station will provide outside and 'off-air' services such as music festivals, job-finding schemes or helplines that give advice and information.

Operating a radio station also requires an extensive administrative staff — receptionists, typists, secretaries, accountants and perhaps a record library co-ordinator. Some stations have a trades union representative who looks after the needs of the staff.

When the station requires extra voices for radio drama production it will employ outside artists. In community radio stations volunteers will help with programmes and extra services like dealing with phone calls and incoming letters. Other volunteers may work on a programme of particular interest to them, for example, for minority ethnic groups. Often these programmes are produced with minimal budgets without paid workers.

In the studio, there is a mixer or control desk that links up the pieces of studio equipment and enables the DJ to control each part of the programme. The control desk links the turntables ('grams) for playing records, cassette machines, open-reel tape machines, telephone selector for phone-in shows, cartridge decks for playing jingles and ads, and microphones for the DJ and other speakers.

The control desk has faders: sliding knobs that control the level of sound. This enables the DJ to adjust the volume in order to talk over the music and also to ensure that sounds are being put out at the same signal level. Each piece of equipment has its own channel and fader on the control desk. The DJ wears headphones ('cans') to line up ('cue') the records before they are played and to hear instructions coming from the producer or the engineer. If items or snippets of information have been pre-recorded, they are played on an open-reel tape player using quarter-inch tape. The sound signals travel from the studio control desk to the control room where the technician makes sure they go to the transmitter at the correct volume and tone.

Extra pre-recorded pieces may be provided by reporters who interview people in the streets, in their own homes, in another studio or over the

Below and **above**   The DJ or presenter sits at the control desk or mixer that links all the equipment for playing tapes, cassettes, cartridges, records and telephone calls. There are also microphones for the presenter and studio guests. Each item of equipment is connected to a channel with separate 'cue' or PFL switches and fader so that, for example, the presenter can talk over background music.

telephone. Interviews in the street that ask various people their views on a particular topic are called 'voxpop' or *vox populi,* meaning 'the voice of the people'. When interview tapes come back to the station, they are transferred or 'dubbed' on to open-reel tape (if they were recorded on a cassette recorder) and edited.

When the various elements of a programme have been assembled a script is written for the DJ or presenter that links all the pieces of interview together. It will also have instructions on when to insert music and sound effects. Script-writing for radio uses familiar, everyday language, short uncomplicated sentences and a straightforward style. A script must be written in such a way that listeners can understand its meaning the first time it is read. The presenter tries to make it sound spontaneous and unrehearsed.

Public, or community, stations around the world are run by teams of volunteers who do everything from cleaning and reception duties to making news and special interest programmes. Volunteers can put across their own points of view within station guidelines and learn a variety of skills. This can mean that women are given the opportunity to learn jobs that are frequently reserved for men in traditionally run stations. For instance, some stations believe the myth that women's voices are too high to be appealing to listeners and rarely employ women broadcasters. Similarly, stations may be reluctant to use broadcasters with a regional accent. Until recently the BBC

A radio journalist edits or 'splices' open-reel tape by adjusting the sound levels and cutting out unwanted material.

John Snagge OBE was a newsreader, announcer and adventurous programme maker for 63 years. For many he was the voice of the BBC.

Above *Outside broadcasts like the BBC Radio 1 Roadshow are linked to the main control desk and allow us to hear 'live' performances.*

did not take on presenters with Irish, Scottish, Welsh, regional or other accents for their national services.

Pirate stations working in the community, such as Peoples Community Radio Line (PCRL) in Birmingham, have large numbers of people involved both in making programmes and running various welfare schemes for local people. PCRL was set up after both of Birmingham's local stations refused airtime for Afro-Caribbean programmes. This pirate station has been raided at least 100 times, has had equipment confiscated and individuals charged under government acts preventing illegal broadcasting. PCRL broadcasters persist in their pirate activity because they feel that the Afro-Caribbean people as well as Asian and Greek communities are not otherwise served. Their aim is eventually to have a licence to broadcast as a local community station.

4 Radio to entertain

Many people tune in to radio to hear music. They can hear records, live or recorded concerts and performances in the studio of music that they might not have in their personal record collections. Music is also used to enhance or link items on other programmes. In fact, music has been so important to radio broadcasting that it has influenced the way radio programming has developed.

As early as the 1920s, the BBC's music programmes were restricted because musicians' unions' rights agreements made them too expensive. Now the BBC pays an annual lump sum to copyright associations in return for a licence to broadcast music. In the early days of radio, the BBC assumed that its role should be to educate its listeners, rather than simply to cater to popular tastes in music. Despite the popularity of American-style music programmes during the Second World War, the BBC was reluctant to play popular music on the radio and it took direct action in the 1960s to change the situation. Pop music pirate stations like Radio Caroline, started by Irish businessman Ronan O'Rahilly, became popular with the public and BBC Radio 1 was set up as a legal alternative.

Music programmes are often 'chance' listening — we're never quite sure what will come next. However, the structure of the music show is not really left to chance; it is usually presented in a fairly defined format. The most commonly known format or type of music

The Radio Big Band, a section of the BBC Radio Orchestra, provided fine music for radio audiences.

programme is a 'Top 40' music show. A disc
jockey (DJ) gives very basic information — the
record name and label, song title and where the
record is placed in the charts. The charts are
lists of those records that are the best sellers
and have the highest airplay ratings for a
particular period.

The DJ also gives time checks, weather and
traffic news, snippets from newspapers, jokes,
horoscope readings, and plays ads, station
promotions and public service announcements.
Interviews in the studio are usually conducted
'live' and are kept to a couple of minutes in
length. Some music shows often feature a

*One of the original DJs on pirate station Radio
Caroline, Canadian Simon Dee, played pop music
and later hosted a TV chat show.*

'personality' DJ such as Steve Wright on BBC
Radio 1. Steve's afternoon show features a
constant stream of music interspersed with
voice caricatures of invented people. Listeners
usually either love or loathe a personality DJ.
Other music shows rely on listener involvement
and may include phone-in dedications or
answers to competitions or quizzes. Request
shows include listeners' letters dedicating
songs to friends or family.

Specialist music programmes are often those played at off-peak times, that is, the less popular listening times when advertising rates are lower. Regulations in Britain and other countries require radio stations to play other music besides the Top 40, so specialist music programmes may feature classical, jazz, reggae, soul, funk, gospel, folk and so on. Specialist music DJs or presenters usually know their subject well and give informed and more detailed comments. Some programmes are presented by low-profile presenters who rarely talk over the faded-down music or give announcements.

Some community stations in the USA and Australia and pirate stations in Britain feature entirely specialist music programmes playing music rarely heard on other stations. Some stations have particular policies about the sort of music that should be played. For example, 3CR in Australia requires that a percentage of the station's music output should be Australian-originated. Other stations believe that shows featuring music originating from Black people should only be presented by Black DJs, many of whom have developed new and original styles of radio presentation.

There are other restrictions covering music programming on all radio stations. The most important is copyright. Almost all records carry the words: 'All rights of the manufacturer and of the owner of the recorded work reserved.

Top 40 radio shows originated from jukeboxes that held just 40 records. As well as playing the Top 40, DJs play ads and jingles and make announcements.

Unauthorized public performance, broadcasting and copying of this record prohibited.' This is to protect the rights of all those involved in making the disc. Radio stations have an agreement to pay a sum of money or percentage of income to be re-distributed to the performer and record company.

Commercial stations pay for the use of records under 'needletime' agreements; the rate of payment is based on their advertising income. Because commercial stations rely on advertising, they aim to attract as large an audience as possible so they can charge high prices for airtime. Even licence-fee funded radio stations must have good audience figures to justify the public money that pays for them. This is why fairly standard formats are used and

Free records are sent to radio stations by record companies who want airplay. Records are stored alphabetically in record libraries.

often predictable 'middle-of-the-road' music heard throughout the day. DJs are given a 'playlist' that details exactly what music they must play with usually a few slots for their own choices. DJs must play ads and announcements and slot in news bulletins exactly in the order and at the times specified on the programme schedule.

Phone-in programmes are an important way of involving listeners in radio. Callers can take part from their own homes, at work or from public telephone boxes and express opinions that may not otherwise be aired. Phone-ins are

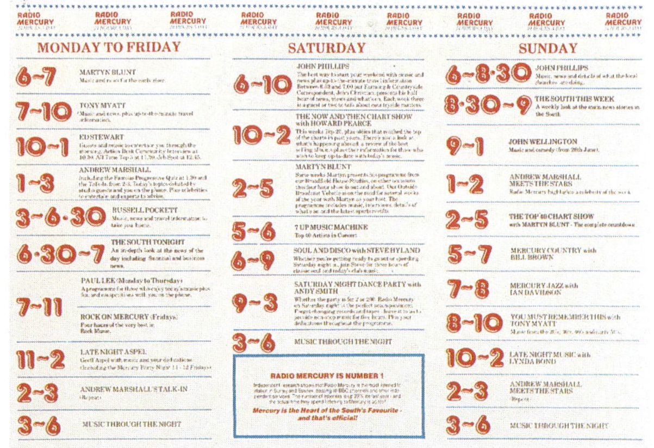

MONDAY TO FRIDAY

6–7 MARTYN BLUNT — Music and news for the early riser.

7–10 TONY MYATT — Music and news, plus up-to-the-minute travel information.

10–1 ED STEWART — Guests and music to entertain you through the morning. Action Desk Community Interviews at 10.30, All Time Top 5 at 11.20, Job Spot at 12.45.

1–3 ANDREW MARSHALL — Including the Famous Progressive Quiz at 1.30 and the Talk-In from 2-3. Today's topics debated by studio guests and you on the phone. Plus celebrities to entertain and experts to advise.

3–6.30 RUSSELL POCKETT — Music, news and travel information to take you home.

6.30–7 THE SOUTH TONIGHT — An in-depth look at the news of the day including financial and business news.

7–11 PAUL LEE (Monday to Thursdays) — A programme for those who enjoy today's music plus fun and competitions with you on the phone.

ROCK ON MERCURY (Fridays) — Four hours of the very best in Rock Music.

11–2 LATE NIGHT ASPEL — Geoff Aspel with music and your dedications (including the Mercury Party Night 11 – 12 Fridays).

2–3 ANDREW MARSHALL'S TALK-IN — (Repeat)

3–6 MUSIC THROUGH THE NIGHT

SATURDAY

6–10 JOHN PHILLIPS — The best way to start your weekend with music and news plus up-to-the-minute travel information. Between 6.30 and 7.00 our Farming & Countryside Correspondent, John Christian, presents his half hour of news, views and what's on. Each week there is a guest or two to talk about countryside matters.

10–2 THE NOW AND THEN CHART SHOW with HOWARD PEARCE — This week's Top 20, plus oldies that reached the top of the charts in past years. There's also a look at what's happening abroad, a review of the best selling albums plus other information for those who wish to keep up-to-date with today's music.

2–5 MARTYN BLUNT — Some weeks Martyn presents his programme from our Broadfield House Studios, on other occasions this four hour show is out and about. Our Outside Broadcast Vehicle is on the road for several weeks of the year with Martyn as your host. The programme includes music, interviews, details of what's on and the latest sports results.

5–6 7 UP MUSIC MACHINE — Top 40 Artists in Concert.

6–9 SOUL AND DISCO with STEVE HYLAND — Whether you're getting ready to go out or spending Saturday night in, join Steve for three hours of classic soul and today's club music.

9–3 SATURDAY NIGHT DANCE PARTY with ANDY SMITH — Whether the party is for 2 or 200, Radio Mercury on Saturday night is the perfect accompaniment. Forget changing records and tapes - leave it to us to provide non-stop music for five hours. Plus your dedications throughout the programme.

3–6 MUSIC THROUGH THE NIGHT

> **RADIO MERCURY IS NUMBER 1**
> Independent research shows that Radio Mercury is the most listened to station in Surrey and Sussex, beating all BBC channels and other independent services. The number of listeners is up 27% on last year, and the total time they spend listening to Mercury is up too!
> *Mercury is the Heart of the South's Favourite - and that's official!*

SUNDAY

6–8.30 JOHN PHILLIPS — Music, news and details of what the local churches are doing.

8.30–9 THE SOUTH THIS WEEK — A weekly look at the main news stories in the South.

9–1 JOHN WELLINGTON — Music and comedy (from 26th June).

1–2 ANDREW MARSHALL MEETS THE STARS — Radio Mercury highlights a celebrity of the week.

2–5 THE TOP 40 CHART SHOW — with MARTYN BLUNT - The complete countdown.

5–7 MERCURY COUNTRY with BILL BROWN

7–8 MERCURY JAZZ with IAN DAVIDSON

8–10 YOU MUST REMEMBER THIS with TONY MYATT — Music from the 50's, 60's, 70's and early 80's.

10–2 LATE NIGHT MUSIC with LYNDA BOND

2–3 ANDREW MARSHALL MEETS THE STARS — (Repeat)

3–6 MUSIC THROUGH THE NIGHT

To meet the demands of different audiences, Radio Mercury's programme schedule includes jazz, soul, rock and disco music.

not entirely spontaneous, however. The programme producer will decide in what order the calls will be taken and cut off those who are abusive, indecent or want to advertise a product. The caller's words are delayed by up to ten seconds before being broadcast so that anything 'inappropriate' can be cut.

An open-line phone-in show can offer airspace for callers to join a discussion on particular issues and the emphasis is on providing entertainment for a wide audience. Other types of phone-in include a studio guest 'expert', aiming to provide advice and information, or feature a celebrity studio guest talking about her or his life and work. Finally, there is the phone-in that discusses callers' personal problems.

Some phone-in presenters have been criticized for their rough and even rude treatment of callers. Presenters have the power to interrupt and to cut off callers, and are often accused of patronizing and mocking callers. Phone-ins can be a medium for the presenters to exhibit their own personalities and views rather than encourage responses from others. Some phone-in shows are run very cheaply, are not well researched and have presenters giving information on topics they know little about. Public and community radio stations in North America and Australia attempt to use phone-ins

The producer of a phone-in programme can cut off a caller whose remarks are abusive, indecent or blatant advertising.

Sue MacGregor, formerly presenter of Woman's Hour. This programme is compiled by a team of producers, researchers and freelance reporters.

in a more balanced way.

While music and phone-in programmes are the most well-known forms of entertainment radio, there are also other forms such as magazine programmes, radio drama and comedy that bring listeners both pleasure and a new perspective.

Magazine programmes usually include a variety of light and serious items. There are news/what's on slots, regular sections for listeners' letters or serialized stories, interviews (both 'live' and pre-recorded) and perhaps short drama or comedy segments, music or voxpops. The programme is often based around a particular theme or idea and has a distinctive title and signature tune. A signature tune is about 30 seconds in length and becomes the recognizable music or sound effects for a particular programme. It is often difficult to define magazine programmes as either entertainment or educative radio. Light entertainment can also be based on serious subjects and deal with them in a serious manner. *Woman's Hour,* running on BBC Radio 4 since 1946, is a well-known magazine programme listened to by many men as well as women.

The variety and quantity of radio drama is often underestimated. On BBC network radio, for example, over 1,000 dramatic productions are broadcast every year. The range of radio drama includes plays, soap operas, story-telling as well as commercials, ads, trailers to advertise special shows coming up, comedy shows and features. Radio can be the vehicle for some brilliant drama, but it is drama of a very particular kind. The 'action' is in what people say as well as in sound effects. Radio drama uses conversations or dialogue as well as monologues very effectively. But the sounds

In the 1930s, BBC sound effects or 'FX' were made in the Effects Studio or gathered on site. Now the BBC has hundreds of sound effects which are available on BBC records.

must be continuous or we may lose track of the story. Sound effects tell us where the characters are: for example, birdsong and wind in trees indicate the countryside. Effects on voices tell us about characters' movements. An echoing voice can tell us that we are in a cave and fading in and out can indicate entrances and exits and the end of a scene.

5 Radio to Educate and Inform

Radio is particularly suitable as a medium to educate and inform. It can cover huge distances, reach many people and does not have the distracting qualities of television when used for direct instruction. Programmes can be *educational*, aiming to impart specific ideas, information or techniques, or *educative*, aiming to inform on a general level. Educative programmes are designed for a wide audience, not just for students. Most radio stations have some commitment to programmes that attempt to inform and educate listeners. These take various forms such as news, current affairs, features and documentaries.

Instant news, like music, is an important function of radio. Because it is voice only, radio news can be relatively simple and cheap to

Educational programmes can be used by individuals who wish to study alone, and can reach many people.

produce. Radio in Britain really developed as a rapid news medium during the Second World War. Before this, radio news was restricted by the Newspaper Proprietors' Association (NPA) who were worried that the BBC would take over the role of newspapers. Similarly, in the USA a press/radio war over news was fought during the 1930s. NPA restrictions were lifted during the General Strike in 1926 and the BBC's reports, despite being broadly pro-government, were a vital channel for news and information to the nation.

In 1936 the Crystal Palace in south London caught fire. Richard Dimbleby, then a young reporter, broadcast a live telephone report from the scene of the fire, well before newspaper reporters could get there. With a background of shouts, firebells and fire crackles, the report showed how quickly and dramatically news could be communicated by radio. This pioneered the news format we now take for granted.

Radio covers a different kind of news from that of newspapers and television. Radio can give only a limited report while newspapers can cover an issue more comprehensively. Radio

Above *When newspapers had closed for the evening, radio news 'scooped' with Richard Dimbleby's telephone coverage of the Crystal Palace fire in 1936.*

Below *News reporting developed during World War Two. This correspondent uses a 'midget' recorder proudly advertised as 'no bigger than a portable gramophone'.*

uses between 160 and 180 words per minute so that a 10-minute bulletin (a considerable coverage to the listener) covers only one or two columns of news copy out of the 30 or 40 in the average newspaper. News on radio cannot be very detailed or complex. However, some news bulletins are followed by extra current affairs and background programmes that cover particular topics more fully.

Radio news cannot be selected according to items of interest by the listener. Rather, the news bulletin is introduced with a headlining 'menu' of what is to come. If the listeners then wish to hear only one item of interest, they must listen to the whole bulletin until the item of interest comes up. Broadcasters use techniques such as 'signposting', with comments like 'Later in the bulletin . . .' or 'Coming up shortly . . .' and 'Flagging' to let us know what subject is coming up next ('Football, and today's game at . . .'). Music, or other sound effects such as pips or tone, indicate the headlines or a new item. Some music stations use music or jingles that repeat the name of the news bulletin. These indicate that this is news and more music will follow.

News is an important part of a station's output. In a radio newsroom the important stories of the day are sorted into order of priority.

Like all radio, the language of news on radio must be kept simple, direct and fairly colloquial or everyday. A news bulletin cannot be re-read or replayed if we did not catch it the first time. There are no visual aids like large headlines, pictures or television images to assist in putting across the message. In radio scripts, sentences are short and words are contracted, for example, 'It's' instead of 'It is'. Headlines are repeated to ensure that we know what is going on and can pick up the story in the middle of the bulletin.

Radio news even on quite different sorts of stations can sound similar. What differentiates one news bulletin from another is the style of presentation — the news reading, extra voices, music or other sound effects. Some newsreaders speak briskly and in an urgent tone while others try to put across a more objective reporting style with a slower, more serious tone. Whatever the style, the newsreader is perceived as a voice of authority. Some advertisers use a news style for their commercials, believing that the serious tone will

Brian Redhead and John Timpson present BBC Radio 4's Today *programme.* Today *has covered news and current affairs each morning for 30 years.*

lend credibility to their product. In Britain, it was not until the Second World War that newsreaders gave their names; this was to prevent the enemy from trying to fake news bulletins. Before that, many listeners thought the BBC news was always read by the same person. Even now, the BBC tends to use readers with similar English accents and authoritative tones.

Most news bulletins include reports from outside news gatherers. International or 'on location' correspondents, specialist editors, interviewers and reporters all provide additional information and comment.

But what exactly is the 'news' and who decides what should be covered and how? Some listeners complain that news coverage is too superficial, not adequately researched and not representative of minority viewpoints and opinions. Media analysts have shown that only certain types of issues are reported on radio news. A 'newsworthy' item must be:

happening at the time of reporting or else a recent event;
dramatic and important (although a dramatic event such as a war is interesting only as long as new stories arise);
clearly understood without complicated explanations;
relevant to our daily lives (a plane crash report will discuss casualties from the radio station's country, even if only a few compared with the number killed from other countries);
fit into our expectations (a peaceful demonstration may not be covered because it was expected to be violent);
able to be continued, that is, a 'running story'.

Above *'Stringers' are correspondents providing international news for specific services. Suwito Yosodipuro reports on Indonesian affairs.*

Below *Robin Day presents BBC Radio 4's* World At One *programme which analyses news with interviews, correspondents' reports and commentary.*

THE WEATHER

Mostly clear tonight and Tuesday, continued cool tonight, with light frost. Slowly rising temperature Tuesday.

Detailed report on Page 29

THE EVENING SUN

Vol. 58 — PAID CIRCULATION SEPTEMBER — MORNING 130,911 EVENING 180,925 — 311,836 — SUNDAY 207,097 | BALTIMORE, MONDAY, OCTOBER 31, 1938 | Entered as second-class matter at Baltimore Postoffice | 30 Pages | 2 Cents

RADIO SCARE BRINGS U. S. PROBE

2 WOMEN DEAD IN CAR CRASH AT SUITLAND, MD.

Washingtonians Killed As Auto Leaves Road And Hits Tree

Husband Of One Blames Lights Of Approaching Machine

Two Washington (D. C.) women were killed early today when the automobile in which they were riding swerved from the road at Suitland, Md., and crashed into a tree.

The dead are:

Mrs. Roma Vaccaro, 22, 222 Eleventh street, southeast.

Mrs. Anna Vaccaro, 68, same address.

According to police, the car was driven by Vincent Vaccaro, husband of the younger woman. All three were taken to the Casualty Hospital in Washington by the members of the Bladensburg rescue squad.

The accident happened near the Cedar Hill Cemetery. Vaccaro said he had been blinded by the lights of an approaching automobile.

Members of the rescue squad said Vaccaro was dead on the way to the hospital. Mrs. Anna Vaccaro, the mother of the driver, died in the hospital. Vaccaro was treated for lacerations of the left arm.

Bus And Car Collide

Forty persons, passengers on a downtown-bound bus, were shaken up during the morning rush hour today when it and a private automobile collided at Fremont and Lexington streets.

The collision occurred where the two streets come together between Carollton and Stricker streets. According to Patrolman William H. Hansen, of the Central district, both vehicles were southbound on Fayette street when the automobile attempted to make a right-hand turn into Lexington street.

The machine was driven by John P. Carson, of 802 Monroe avenue, and the bus by Edward L. Prokuski, of 2217 East Fairmount avenue, according to police. Patrolman Hansen was summoned to Traffic Court to answer charges of reckless driving.

Three Hurt On Motor Cycle

Three youths were injured, one seriously, when the motorcycle on which they were riding on the Leonardtown Pike failed to negotiate a turn near Charlotte Hall and left the road.

All three were taken to the Casualty Hospital, where they were identified as John Burger, 22, and Lloyd Riggs, 21, both of Benedict, Md., and Vincent Knowlton, of Washington.

Burger, the driver, was said to be suffering from a fracture of the skull. Riggs and Knowlton were treated for lacerations and internal injuries. Patrolman Thomas Farrell, of the Waldorf substation of the Maryland State Police, is investigating the accident.

Car Plunges 30 Feet

Mrs. Anna Conlon, 31, of Lane avenue, was treated at St. Agnes Hospital today after the car in which she was riding plunged 30 feet...

[Continued On Page 15, Column 1]

On The INSIDE

Race Results and entries will be found in this edition

On Page 23

Here's A Diet Story, But Without A Woman In It

JOHN TURNER, JR.   H. LINDBERG

Jockeys Converging On Pimlico Have To Watch Food To Keep Weight Down—All Except F. A. Smith, Who Can't Get Over 95

Here is a diet story without a woman in it.

A group of young men who keep a sharper eye on their weights than a Hollywood movie queen, but who don't do it for the sake of appearance, move into their usual quarters at Pimlico with the opening of the fall races there tomorrow.

With a few exceptions, the boys can't take a potato in the face, and a dish of spaghetti is something they prefer not to think about.

May Mean Money

These young men are, of course, the jockeys who will pilot the thoroughbreds around the big oval during the thirteen-day meeting. Ounces of flesh on eight riders mean the difference between victory or defeat in close finishes, and a consequent difference in the amount of money each rider can bank at the end of the day.

These riders, in as far as weight maintenance goes, fall mainly into three categories or combinations thereof:

First, the "miss a meal" type is a boy who doesn't have a great deal of trouble making weight, but who goes in to a mount requiring two or three pounds less than he normally weighs, but just stops eating until the weight disappears.

Some Are Serious Type

Second, the seriously dieting type who passes up the bread, potatoes, spaghetti and fat meals at every meal.

Third, the rider who dons his rubber suit and sweatshirts and takes to the long grind — running around the track until the surplus weight comes off.

Then there is a fourth type to unusual as to be spectacular. In the boy who needs more weight, but can't put it on. Such a case is the E. R. Bradley rider F. A. Smith. His weight is 95 pounds. He eats all the things they cram into him...

[Continued On Page 10, Column 1]

DIES CHARGES PWA HALTED TEXAS JOBS

Says He Can't Prove Cancellations Were Due President's Disapproval Of Probe

[By the Associated Press]

Washington, Oct. 31 — Chairman Martin Dies (Dem., Texas) of a House committee investigating un-American activities said today two public works projects in his district had been cancelled since the committee inquiry began.

He added, however, that he was not prepared to charge that the cancellations were due to the Administration's disapproval of the methods of the committee.

Dam Job Canceled

President Roosevelt said recently the committee had permitted itself to be used for political purposes that were un-American. The committee also has been criticized by Secretary of Interior Harold Ickes the PWA Administrator, and by Secretary of Labor Frances Perkins.

Dies said one of the projects for a $12,000,000 dam at Rockland, Texas, was cancelled soon after the investigation began.

He showed reporters a copy of a letter dated October 25, in which George M. Bull, PWA regional director, had notified B. T. McWhorter, Jr., of Port Arthur, Texas, that a grant for a Port Arthur causeway had been recommended.

Charges Pressure Used

McWhorter is chairman of the Port Arthur Bridge Commission.

Dies said he was prepared to establish that the Administration had used pressure to obtain time for...

[Continued On Page 15, Column 1]

ROOSEVELT URGES DOWNEY ELECTION

Writes California Senate Candidate Is "Real Liberal In Mind And Heart"

[By the Associated Press]

Los Angeles, Oct. 31 — President Roosevelt entered the California political scene today with a written endorsement of Sheridan Downey, Democratic candidate for United States Senator, who war termed "a real liberal in mind and heart."

Downey headquarters released a letter the President sent to Congressman Jerry Voorhis in which it said:

"You know how deeply I feel about the necessity of having representative tives in the Congress who will face present-day problems with present-day philosophy. It would be a calamity for California to be represented in the Senate by a dyed-in-the-wool reactionary."

Called "Real Liberal"

"I am convinced that Sheridan is a real liberal in mind and in heart, and would ably and constructively represent the predominant liberal thought of your State."

Downey, with support from the $30 every-Thursday pension movement, won in the Democratic primary against Senator William G. McAdoo who had been publicly urged by the President to seek re-election.

Downey's Republican opponent is Philip Bancroft, farmer-lawyer.

Service; For Mrs. Harris

Atlanta, Oct. 31 — Six grandsons were chosen pallbearers for the funeral of Mrs. Esther Lanoue Harris, widow of the creator of the "Uncle Remus" Negro folk tales, Joel Chandler Harris, at the Sacred Heart Church here today. They were John C. Harris Jr, Lucien Harris Jr, Remus Harris, Fitz Wagner and Richard Henry Wright, Mrs Harris, 84, died Saturday night at the home of a daughter, Mrs. Edwin Camp in Atlanta.

ENGLISH CABINET SHAKEN UP AS DEFENSE MOVE

Sir John Anderson, Once Bengal Administrator, New Lord Privy Seal

Runciman, Mediator In Prague, Is Lord President Of Council

[By the Associated Press]

London, Oct. 31 — Sir John Anderson, broad-shouldered administrator who crushed terror in Bengal between 1932 and 1937, today was appointed Lord Privy Seal in a Cabinet shakeup believed to be preparatory to a widespread organization of the nation for defense.

Viscount Runciman, who tried in vain to mediate in the crisis which led to Germany's absorption of Czechoslovakia's Sudetenland, was named Lord President of the Council.

MacDonald Gains Post

Malcolm MacDonald, already Secretary for Colonies, was given the additional post of Dominions Secretary.

The post of Lord Privy Seal became vacant last week when Earl de la Warr was shifted to the Ministry of Education. Runciman succeeds Viscount Hailsham, who resigned. The dominions post has been vacant since the death of Lord Stanley October 16.

Denies Difference Of Opinion

In his letter of resignation Lord Hailsham said he was quitting in order to put at the Prime Minister's disposal a post which does not involve the administration of any great department of the State, and so give any other opportunity of a wider reinforcement of the Cabinet.

He emphasized that his resignation was not due to any differences with Chamberlain on policy or opinion.

Sidetracked Out Rebellion

Ordinarily the post of Lord Privy Seal is a sinecure, but Anderson, with a reputation for drive and administrative ability, is expected to be given the job of putting Air Raid Precautions, the Government bureau in charge of civilian preparations, on a sound footing.

He is a long-time civil servant, was formerly permanent Under Secretary of State in the Home Office, and turned to national politics after returning from Bengal last year. He is 56 years old.

In Bengal he stamped out terror and rebellion ruthlessly, although there were three attempts to assassinate him.

Mends Full Cabinet

Prime Minister Neville Chamberlain today met his full Cabinet to draft his program for Parliament soon beginning tomorrow which was to deal chiefly with home policy and diplomacy.

The Prime Minister's chief ministers were how to reconcile Ministerial differences over rearmament and how to allay national apprehension over admitted defense deficiencies. He presided at a meeting of the "inner Cabinet," before the full Cabinet met.

"Grand Inquest" Likely

Three Ministers—War Secretary Leslie Hore-Belisha, Home Secretary Sir Samuel Hoare and Air Minister Sir Kingsley Wood—were said to want creation of a Ministry of Supplies with compulsory powers to effect the arms speed-up, but Chamberlain was opposed to this plan on the ground that it would dislocate industry and prejudice export trade.

Nurse Defends U. S. Agent Accused By Spy Witness

Says Her Testimony That He Told Her She Might Leave Country While Under Subpœna Was Misinterpreted

[By the Associated Press]

New York, Oct. 31 — Kate Moog, buxom blonde who had been told by spying as a Government witness today testifying from the German spy trial, said former Federal Agent Leon G. Turrou had impressed her with the seriousness of the case and with the necessity of being here.

The young nurse, owner of a convalescent home in Manhattan, denied that anyone had told her she might leave the country while she was under subpœna.

Accused By Woman

Counsel for Johanna Hofmann, one of the three defendants on trial, had accused Turrou of letting Dr Ignatz T Griebl slip away...

Miss Moog testified Friday that Dr...

30 Baltimoreans Phone Jersey In 'War' Fright

Realistic Radio Play Also Causes Rash Of City Calls, Many Humorous Incidents

Eighty long-distance calls were made within twenty minutes last night by apprehensive Baltimoreans to friends or information centers at Newark N. J., after listeners here had heard a portion of a broadcast dramatization of H. G. Wells' fantastic story, "The War of the Worlds."

In the city telephone switchboards on all exchanges flared with an unprecedented number of Sunday evening calls. The same twenty-minute period saw 200 extra calls clearing through the telephone company's information bureau, and more than 2,100 calls over the normal number registered in the city's residential section.

One Man Runs Two Miles

All across the State there were reports of terror that stalked by night following the fantastic broadcast by Orson Welles and his Mercury Theater. One Baltimore countian ran about two miles from Rockdale to Hebbville to bring home his wife, who had been visiting.

An Eastern Shore correspondent telegraphed that mass hysteria had gripped the town of Preston. A judge residing there, he said, after warning his friends of impending catastrophe called the State police at Easton and told them the story.

Police Reassure Judge

As it happened, the police in that substation had been listening to the program and were able to reassure the official.

At the Sunpapers, the night telephone operators attempted vainly to tabulate calls from frightened and hysterical city residents. After recording 550, however, they had to stop counting and turn their entire attention to answering the queries. They had no opportunity to rest until well after midnight.

Humorous incidents by the score were told and retold today, many of them growing with each repetition.

Whole Neighborhood Upset

The broadcast caused commotion and plenty of loss of sleep in the 3900 block of Morris Pleasant avenue. One woman resident of the block described the uproar in the neighborhood after she and her husband and their 3-year-old son returned from a drive.

"Our oldest son, he's 26 years old, met us at the front door, shouting 'The world is coming to an end! I just heard it on the radio!'"

Husband Convinced

"My husband didn't believe it at first, but he began listening to the radio and then he got all excited and started yelling. Our son jumped up and ran out and my husband ran out after him because he didn't say where he was going.

"After a while he came back and said he'd called up his girl in Dundalk to tell her to watch the clouds of black smoke, that the end of the world would come when they reached here.

"My husband came back and grabbed the coffee pot to make some coffee. We were all drinking coffee, my hand got to laughin and laughing and I couldn't stop, I kept the world was..."

[Continued On Page 11, Column 1]

Excerpts From Broadcast Play That Panicked Nation

Dance Program Interrupted For "News Report" Of Explosions On Mars, Then Steel Tubes Fall In Jersey, Slaughter Begins

[By the Associated Press]

New York, Oct. 31 — Here is an outline of the radio broadcast that panicked the nation last night.

After an introductory explanation by Orson Welles, an announcer gave a commonplace weather forecast. Then, in the standard fashion, came the words: "We take you now to the — Hotel, where we will hear the music of," etc.

Routine Beginning

The program opened with a routine announcement that another of the Mercury Theater of the Air's radio dramatizations—H. G. Wells' novel—was about to be presented.

The drama began with dance music which was interrupted after a few seconds with a breath-taking announcement in news-broadcast tempo:

"We interrupt our program of dance music to bring you a special bulletin from the intercontinental radio news," it said.

"Explosions On Mars"

"Twenty minutes before 8 Professor Farrell, of the Mount Jennings Observatory, Chicago, Ill., reports observing several explosions of incandescent gas occurring at regular intervals on the planet Mars.

"An object was reported 'moving toward the earth with enormous velocity, 'like a jet of blue gas shot from a gun.

"We return you now to our New York studio," the drama continued.

Scene Turns To Princeton

A moment after the buildup announcement of gas explosions on Mars the scene of the fantasy switched to Princeton, where an astronomer undertook to "explain" the phenomena.

Another meteor "struck" at nearby Grover's Mill. In interrupt the proceedings the announcer "struck dumb," who rushed out with the air of a touchdown run.

It was a great tube of metal then reported not a meteor at all.

"This Is Terrific"

"Just a minute," the announcer added. "Something's happening! Ladies and gentlemen, this is terrific.

"The end of the thing is beginning to come off. The top is beginning to..."

[Continued On Page 10, Column 3]

Excuse It Please

Gridder Who Left Bench To Tackle Runner Is "Awfully Sorry"

Cincinnati, Oct. 31 (AP)—Remorseful John Bannon, of the Providence College football team, was as bewildered as anyone else today by his blind leap from the bench to tackle Xavier University's quarterback, Tom Hogan, on a touchdown run.

The Providence center wandered around the clubhouse afterward as if he could not quite understand what made him do it. He only asked 'Why did this have to happen to me?' All he reported not a meteor at all.

Officials gave the touchdown to Xavier. Xavier then went ahead to a victory across the continent.

M'NINCH CALLS INVASION PANIC "REGRETTABLE"

Orders CBS To Supply Script And Recording Of Fantasy

Thousands, Terrified By "News Flashes," Come Out Of Hiding

Wells Is Upset

New York, Oct. 31 (AP) — Jacques Chambrun, literary representative for H. G. Wells, today said the British author was "deeply concerned" that the radio dramatization of his book should have spread alarm in this country.

Chambrun said Wells cabled him from London this morning, declaring that "the Columbia Broadcasting System and Mr Orson Welles have far overstepped their rights in the matter ... and should make a full retraction."

He said Wells cabled that the radio dramatization was made "with a liberty that amounts to a complete rewriting" and made Wells' novel into "an entirely different story." Chambrun said the author considered it a "totally unwarrantable liberty."

[By the Associated Press]

Washington, Oct. 31 — The Federal Communications Commission today began an investigation of a dramatic radio broadcast which led some people to believe last night that men from Mars had attacked the United States.

Chairman Frank P. McNinch asked the Columbia Broadcasting System to furnish the commission with the script of the dramatized version of H. G. Wells' "War of the Worlds."

Thousands of persons believed the drama to be authentic news reports.

Gets Many Phone Calls

McNinch said he had received many telephone calls last night about the broadcast, but that the commission had received only ten telegrams, all protesting, up to this forenoon.

He issued this statement:

"I have this morning requested the Columbia Broadcasting Company to telegraph to forward to us a complete stenographic transcription of the 'War of the Worlds' which was broadcast last night and which, by those indicated, caused widespread excitement, terror and fright. I shall request prompt consideration of this matter by the commission.

"Regrettable," He Says

"I withhold final judgment until later, but any broadcast that creates such general panic and fear as this one is reported to have done is, to say the least, regrettable

"The widespread public reaction to this broadcast, as indicated by the press, is another demonstration of the power and force of radio and points again the serious public responsibility of those who are licensed to operate stations."

Commissioner T A M Craven said the commission should proceed with great caution so as not to take any action which would impede radio's being used for development of the dramatic arts.

Opposes Censorship

Warning against any attempt at "censoring what shall or shall not be said over the radio" he added:

"I do not believe satisfied regulation of poor service necessarily constitutes grounds for the revocation of the license of a station. This does not apply to criminal offenses."

"The public does not want a spineless radio."

Some Want Play Repeater

Station WJSV, the Washington outlet for Columbia, said it received about 200 telephone calls today in connection with the broadcast. Five out of six, officials said, were requests that it be repeated tonight.

Communications Commissioner Paul A Walker said:

"This incident illustrates the need for radio being in the hands of persons with proper judgment, proper service of the fitness of things in this fine sense of the qualities of broadcasting programs."

Thousands of listeners throughout the country fled from their homes in terror last night when they tuned in on the synthetic news broadcast which predicted the war between interplanetary war.

The bulletins became so realistic that they sent a wave of mass hysteria across the continent.

Explanatory announcements during...

[Continued On Page 14, Column 2]

Frequently news items chosen are negative, reporting crime or disaster, and lead us to feel that all news is depressing. News for local stations often comes through a networked news service or agency. This means that it cannot be as local as that gathered by the station itself. Local radio stations still rely on network news because it saves them the cost of journalists' salaries and news expenses.

Recognizing these problems, alternative news agencies have been set up. In Australia, the National Program Service (NPS) compiles and redistributes news and current affairs material. The Pacifica Foundation in the USA links five community broadcasting stations that aim to give access to ideas generally absent from the media. Pacifica networks news, Developing World programming, public affairs, drama and literature, music and women's news. Also the Women's International News Gathering Service, or WINGS, compiles and distributes news by and about women with the aim of getting more news of women on the air. While news and current affairs programmes are the most obvious, there are other forms of educative and informative radio, such as magazine programmes, features, documentaries, social action broadcasting and schools radio.

Feature and documentary programmes allow the broadcaster creative ways to cover a significant event or point of view. Documentaries are generally based on evidence such as written records, named sources and interviews, whereas features are not necessarily honest, balanced or factual reporting. They may use folk songs, poetry, fictional drama or sound effects to create impressions and depict atmosphere and mood. Both forms can merge into the other, so that while, for instance, we may not know all the details of Captain Cook's voyages to Australasia, we can put together a drama based on his diaries, his companions' diaries, the ships' logs and so on. While this idea could still be a feature, it is based on fact.

It is important that we as listeners are not deceived into thinking that an account of a current issue is factual when it is not. In New York in 1939, the H. G. Wells novel *War of the Worlds* was adapted for radio by Orson Welles. A fake news bulletin announced a Martian invasion and terrified thousands of radio listeners who panicked to escape from the city. The reaction to this radio drama which was imitating the news/documentary format, gives an idea of how, without sufficient information, listeners can be misled. Some media theorists have assumed from this incident that radio listeners are easily persuaded and do not make informed choices about how they use radio. In fact, listeners use radio for various purposes as we saw in the introduction. One way to use radio is to take part in making radio programmes and to learn how radio operates. In Britain, one way to do this is through Social Action Broadcasting (SAB) projects.

Social Action Broadcasting is defined as broadcasting that tackles problems that affect people's lives. It involves non-professionals in making programmes and gives them access to airtime and encourages local people to participate in community radio services. SAB projects often cover adult literacy, women's health, youth unemployment programmes, telephone helplines, appeals and information slots. The SAB programmes are also backed-up with written material that gives further advice and information. Many projects operate with volunteers who are able to learn skills. Using volunteers for certain SAB programmes and slots has been criticized, however, particularly where station income is earned by unpaid workers but goes into station shareholders' pockets. SAB complements Britain's public service broadcasting requirements by providing material for local stations, but critics of the practice say that the material should not be broadcast in token SAB slots but should be a large part of the stations' output.

In Britain, BBC schools radio provides programmes on subjects such as computers, careers and microtechnology. The Open University offers audio and video tapes for students and teachers. A new programme for primary schools, called *In The News*, has also just been introduced, aiming to present current news in terms that children can understand without needing background knowledge.

Left *In 1939,* The Evening Sun *in Baltimore reported the widespread panic among listeners of* The War of the Worlds *radio drama.*

Since 1967, student radio stations have been broadcasting legally within British college and university campuses. Although mainly used for music programmes, these stations are also used by media students to produce educational broadcasting. In the USA and Australia, public stations have arisen from schools and colleges and can broadcast to local communities outside the campuses. Other stations may broadcast programmes by students who produce radio programmes instead of writing essays as part of their English, science, social studies and languages classes. Also in Australia, special two-way radio equipment allows children in remote areas to come into contact with teachers and students through 'Schools of the Air'. Since

Schooling for these Aymara Indians in remote areas of southern Peru can be provided by radio schools and correspondence classes.

1951, these schools have developed to complement correspondence courses and cover thousands of square miles of sparsely populated regions.

Another form of educational broadcasting is specifically designed for societies that include people of different cultural and ethnic backgrounds. Bilingual programmes use more than one language and provide radio for those who speak little or no English. They also aim to encourage English-speaking listeners to learn about other cultures.

6 Broadening Horizons

So far we have looked at forms of national and local radio. What we have not talked about is radio exchanges on a worldwide basis and why these are important.

During the period of experimentation in radio early this century, most of the industrialized nations established radio services that could frequently be received by other countries but were primarily intended for listeners within the country of origin. In 1927, the first more or less continuous broadcast service for listeners overseas was established in Holland to serve its far-flung colonial empire. Other countries soon followed suit. After the use of international radio for propaganda purposes during the Second World War, many countries developed radio services aimed at spreading political opinions either through obvious messages or more subtle programmes that showed how attractive life under a particular government could be. Voice Of America is an international service provided by the USA and has a network of 101 transmitters (68 overseas) broadcasting 900 hours of programming weekly in 38 languages. Programmes frequently reflect government trends and changes in policy. Most foreign programming in the USSR was blocked by government authorities but some of these restrictions have recently been lifted.

In Britain, the BBC has an External Services Unit that broadcasts programmes in English and other languages to foreign countries. The BBC World Service also broadcasts a varied diet of news, current affairs and topical programmes as well as features, music and drama. An international phone-in produced with BBC Radio 4 called *It's Your World* features people talking from all over the world. The BBC's Topical Tapes Unit provides weekly taped programmes for use by broadcasters internationally. Current affairs material is also fed via satellite to National Public Radio in Washington and to the Australian Broadcasting Commission and Radio New Zealand three times a week.

In the USA, Canada, Britain, Australia and other wealthy countries, communication by satellite is rapidly developing. Radio signals and TV pictures are sent to a satellite orbiting in space and rotating at the same speed as the earth. The satellite receives signals via one frequency from a large dish aerial at an earth station and then transmits them back to another frequency. The signals are received by a small dish aerial individually owned by a listener/viewer, café or pub manager, or by a local community dish aerial or cable TV station. Direct Broadcasting by Satellite (DBS) can offer clearer pictures and stereo sound for television, other data services as well as high quality radio broadcasts for people wherever they live.

For less-developed countries, international services offer both joys and problems. While programmes from other countries give a greater

Sue MacGregor presented It's Your World, *a programme that invited callers from around the world to discuss international issues, such as terrorism.*

variety to the local radio diet, they often contrast sharply with local radio material and give an idealized picture of the countries that produced them. These imported programmes are usually made on relatively large budgets with highly-trained staff and good technical resources; consequently, they seem better made and more attractive than local programming. Importing programmes can be cheaper than training staff and buying equipment for local material, so the medium is often dominated by foreign material. Developing countries cannot yet afford to use satellite and by the time they can, it may be that all the prime sites and frequencies will be owned by wealthy countries and media entrepreneurs producing a bland international style of programming. With the possibility of covering the world with satellite broadcasts, the proposed diet of programmes to suit people wherever they are is a concern for everyone.

At present, satellite technology is still at an experimental stage, and regulation and

Above *Telecommunications satellites orbiting in space allow radio signals to be sent from one country to another almost simultaneously.*

Below *Many developing countries are concerned that their native music is ignored while young people listen to Western countries' pop music.*

monitoring of stations, finance, ownership and programming policies have not been sorted out. It is to be hoped that media entrepreneurs who already own large proportions of the newspaper, independent radio and cable TV industries do not step in to take over satellite communication without some form of accountability to listeners and viewers.

In order to ensure that people get what they want from the medium, listeners need to have more control over radio. In Britain, after many years of campaigning for changes in radio, a parliamentary discussion document (known as a 'Green Paper') recently suggested that the Home Office license hundreds of new local radio stations and three independent national radio stations. While this would open up the choice of radio in Britain on a par with the USA and Australia, these opportunities have been offered only to commercial operators, that is, ·people whose main interest is to make money rather than provide the various sorts of programmes and stations people have indicated that they want to hear.

There are no radio stations in Britain whose profits go back to the station rather than to individual shareholders or owners. Nor are there currently any stations operating with financial support from listener supporters, local councils, trade unions, education authorities or any other public bodies. This means that stations that wish to offer minority, local or experimental programming will have to struggle to make money from specialist markets in competition with other more general operators. Examples from around the world, such as the public radio stations in Australia and community broadcasters in the USA, show some success among stations supported by listeners and local organizations, but all these stations have some support from government funds as well.

Communications mogul Australian-born Rupert Murdoch has part-ownership in an international chain of newspapers, television and radio stations, and interests in cable TV and satellite.

Listeners can influence radio broadcasting in two ways. They can demand that existing stations serve local communities more effectively, or establish their own radio stations. Britain's pirate stations have demonstrated that radio can be cheap and easy to set up. 'Radio Arthur' jammed a local radio station during the coal miners' strike in 1984 to put across alternative news and urge listeners to save mines and support the striking miners. However, in 1984, the Telecommunications Act made it easier for government agencies to track down and confiscate the equipment of illegally broadcasting pirate stations.

There is a history of piracy in other countries where local people struggle to put across alternative viewpoints. At present in El Salvador, the war between the American-backed government troops and local guerrilla forces is reported by two illegal radio stations, Radio

Phone-in presenter Brian Hayes prepares to interview the National Union of Mineworkers leader, Arthur Scargill, on London's independent station LBC, during the 1984 miners' strike.

Farabundo Marti and Radio Venceremos. The stations are constantly on the move, giving reports on the war from a point of view not heard on government radio. They also provide programmes on literacy, health and trade union issues.

If listeners want to change radio they can complain about programmes that insult or offend them and praise programmes that give local, well-produced views. Certain programmes are specially designed to put across listeners' opinions. Listeners can also put forward proposals for new licence applications. Many people want to ensure that there are limits on non-local material and a fixed minimum quota of well-made programmes covering experimental and minority interests. Research in London's Tower Hamlets district, for example, records the wishes of some Somali women to produce local news that would be gathered in people's homes specifically for the Somali community.

Some people may have ideas and proposals for completely different programmes. One way to put these new ideas across is to become involved in a local station and learn how to make programmes. Hospital, student and different kinds of local stations always welcome volunteers. Also, with some basic equipment, a helpful teacher and the school public address system, students can start their own radio station to 'broadcast' during breaks.

Radio is an important way to make our voices heard in societies, whether democratic or not, where broadcasting is dominated by commercial or non-elected bodies. To leave it to these groups is to deny ourselves access to an important communication medium.

Illegally broadcasting Radio Farabundo Marti moves around El Salvador to report on the war between government troops and local guerrilla forces and to educate listeners on health and local issues.

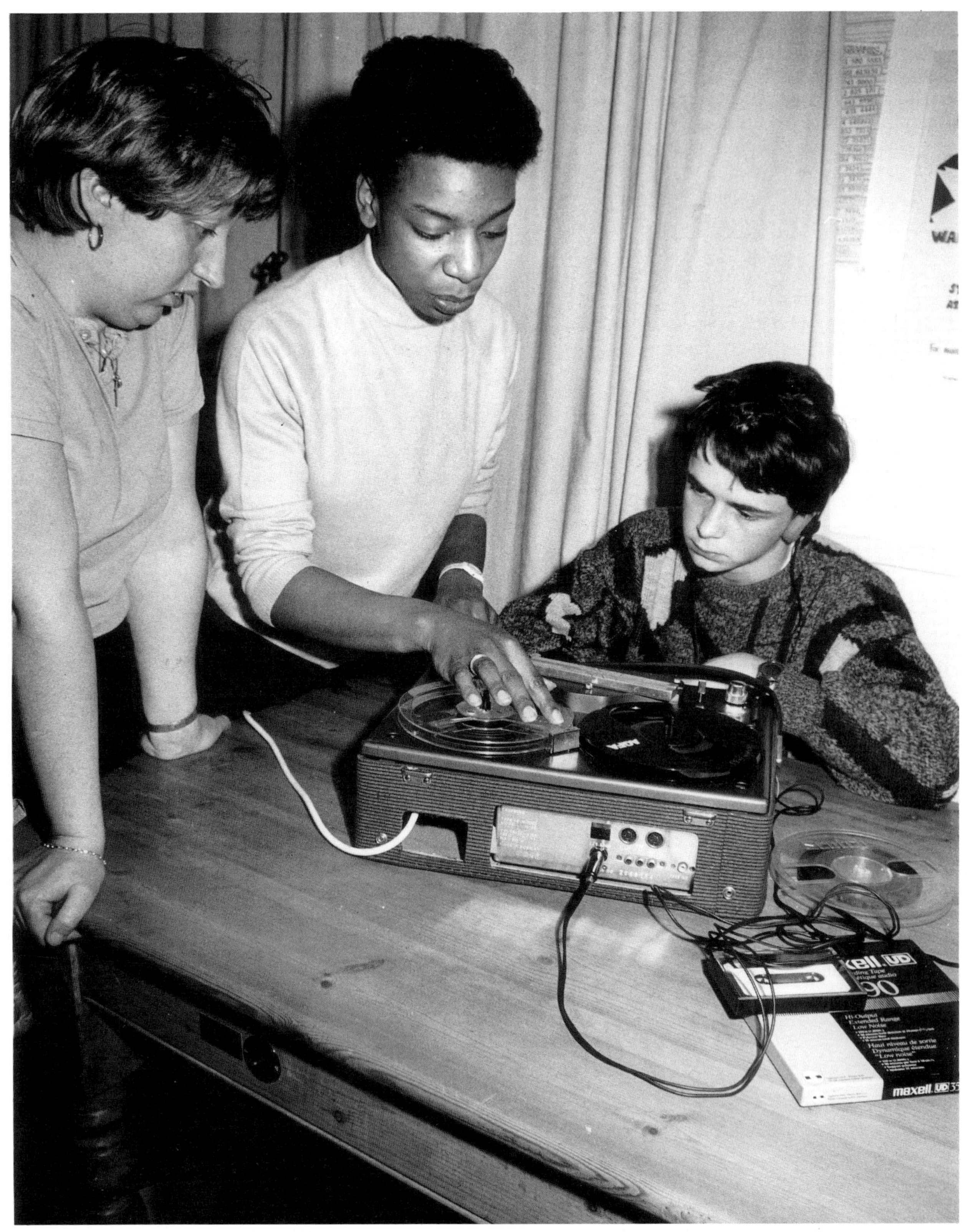

A community radio training project on a large housing estate in south-east London, where local people can learn communication skills with a view to setting up their own radio station.

Glossary

ABC Australian Broadcasting Commission, which produces and broadcasts programmes on radio and television.

ABT Australian Broadcasting Tribunal, which grants licences to broadcast.

Actuality Sound recorded at the actual location.

Audience research Studies of radio audiences — their likes, dislikes, times they listen, and so on.

BBC British Broadcasting Corporation, which produces and broadcasts programmes on radio and television.

Bilingual programmes Programmes in two languages.

Cable radio Radio stations that 'broadcast' via cables connected to the homes they serve.

Commercials Advertisements.

Copyright The exclusive right, enforced by law for a specific period, of an author, composer, musician etc. over the broadcast, or any other use, of his or her original work. Copyrighted material needs the permission of the copyright holder to be broadcast.

Correspondent A person who provides radio stations with news information.

Documentary A programme that gives factual information.

Dubbing Transferring sound from one tape to another.

Edit To cut out, add to or re-arrange parts of recorded material in order to make a radio programme.

Engineer A person who is responsible for the technical aspects of radio broadcasting.

Fader A sliding knob on a mixer that adjusts the level of the sound signal.

FCC Federal Communications Commission (USA), which allocates frequencies to stations and awards licences to broadcast.

Feature programme A programme that tells a story or makes a point using creative, imaginative radio techniques such as music or poetry.

Flagging Giving a short indication of what the next item will be.

IBA Independent Broadcasting Authority (British), which rents transmitters and awards franchises to companies to run radio and television stations.

Light entertainment Programmes such as popular music and drama, serialized stories and comedy.

Mixer Part of the control desk, which links up all the pieces of equipment in the studio for co-ordinated signal and ease of use.

NFCB National Federation of Community Broadcasters (USA), a support organization for community radio stations.

Off-air services Help offered by the radio station for the community finding jobs, homes, giving advice, etc.

Pre-recorded Material recorded before being played; not live.

PSA Public Service Announcement made free of charge for the benefit of the community.

Researcher The person who finds all the background material for programmes.

SAB Social Action Broadcasting (Britain). Programmes trying to help solve people's problems.

Script Written schedule of everything that will be heard on the programme.

Serial Novel or story that is rewritten for radio and read in shorter pieces at a regular time.

Signature tune Recognizable music that introduces a particular show.

Signposting In news, to let the listener know what is coming up next.

Soap opera A continuous drama based on the everyday events of a particular community.

Transistors Elements in radio receivers that amplify the sound.

Transmitter Sends signals from the studio to the transmitting aerial to be radiated via radio waves.

Two-way Radio that can be received and sent.

Booklist

Helen Baehr and Michelle Ryan *Shut Up and Listen! Women and Local Radio* (Comedia, 1984)

P. Cohen and C. Gardner (eds.) *It Ain't Half Racist, Mum: Fighting Racism in the Media* (Comedia, 1982)

Andrew Crissel *Understanding Radio* (Methuen, 1986)

James Curran (ed.) *Bending Reality* (Pluto Press, 1986)

Alex Dix *The Australian Broadcasting Commission in Review, National Broadcasting in the 1980s* Volume 2 Report (1981)

Jane Drinkwater *Get It On Radio and Television: A Practical Guide to Getting Airtime* (Pluto Press, 1984)

Glasgow University Media Group *Really Bad News* (Writers & Readers, 1982)

John Hind & Stephen Mosco *Rebel Radio: The Full Story of British Pirate Radio* (Pluto Press, 1985)

L. W. Lichty & M. C. Topping *American Broadcasting: A Source Book on the History of Radio and Television* (Hastings House, 1976)

Simon Partridge *Not the BBC/IBA: The Case for Community Radio* (Comedia, 1982)

Further Information

UK

Campaign for Press & Broadcasting Freedom
9 Poland Street
London W1   Tel: 01-437 2795
Campaigns for freedom of information on the media. Offers information on trades unions, media analysis groups and has a network of regional offices.

Independent Broadcasting Authority
70 Brompton Road
London SW3 1EY

The Media Project
Volunteer Centre UK
29 Lower Kings Road
Berkhamsted, Herts HP4 2AB   Tel: 04427-73311
Offers support and information on Social Action Broadcasting.

Community Radio Association (CRA)
London Development Unit
South Bank House
Black Prince Road
London SE1 7SJ   Tel: 01-582 7972

Women's Airwaves
90 De Beauvoir Road
London N1 4EL   Tel: 01-241 3729
Feminist programme-making and training collective.

Black Women in Media
c/o Outwrite, Oxford House
Derbyshire Street
London E2.

National Association of Student Broadcasters (NASB)
Chris Martin, Imperial College Radio
Southside, Princes Gardens
London SW7   Tel: 01-589 5111 ext 3440

Relay Radio Magazine and Media Training
Unit 109, Bon Marché
444 Brixton Road
London SW9 8EJ   Tel: 01-274 4000

USA

National Federation of Community Broadcasters (NFCB)
1314 14th Street NW
Washington DC 20005

National Public Radio (NPR)
2025 M Street NW
Washington DC 20036

Pacifica National Office
5316, Venice Boulevard
Los Angeles
CA 90019
Provides information on Pacifica Network stations, program service, radio archive and radio news bureau.

Women's International News Gathering Service (WINGS)
Katherine Davenport, Frieda Werden
PO Box 6758, San Francisco
CA 94101

AUSTRALIA

Australian Broadcasting Commission
Head Office: Broadcast House
145-153 Elizabeth Street
Sydney, NSW 2001

Public Broadcasting Association of Australia (PBAA)
80 George Street
Sydney, NSW 2000

Index

Picture acknowledgements

The author and publishers would like to thank the following for allowing their illustrations to be reproduced in this book: BBC Enterprises 8, 11 (bottom), 23 (top), 24, 30; BBC Hulton Picture Library 9, 32 (bottom); Capital Radio 16 (bottom); Darce Cassidy (3CR) 13 (left), 17; John Frost Historical Newspaper Service 36; Abel Lagos 44; South American Pictures (Marian Morrison) 38; Christine Osborne 15 (top); Popperfoto 10 (left), 11 (top), 25; RFM Support Group 43; Paul Seheult *cover,* 15 (bottom), 18 (both), 19, 20, 21, 22, 26, 27, 28 (both); Topham Picture Library 6, 7, 12 (bottom), 23 (bottom), 29, 32, (top), 33, 34, 35 (bottom), 39, 41, 42; ZEFA 4, 12 (top), 14 (both), 31, 40 (both).
All other pictures from the Wayland Picture Library.
The publishers would also like to thank the staff at Radio Mercury in Crawley for their help and co-operation.